Athlete 25 Project

Any athlete, any age, any sport...

ISBN-13: 978-1522827184
ISBN-10: 1522827188

Special thanks to:

My family, for making me feel like I am someone,

Jena, my wife, for supporting my crazy ideas and post-it rampages,

Life, for teaching me about itself through sport,

And God for giving me something to believe in.

Table of Contents

PART IV - EDUCATIONAL

PART V - MENTAL

Introduction

The Athlete25 Project is exactly what it says, a project. People will doubt, people will disagree, and that is okay. However, I challenge you to try it. Take each topic and work at it, give an honest effort. Be receptive to the learning process that will occur. This project is about learning; it's about expanding yourself as a coach or an athlete. A good athlete is always trying to do something to get better, a great athlete perfects these areas.

When going through the school system colleges look for well-rounded individuals mixing educational achievements with athletic accomplishments. They look at the bigger picture of the person, what have they done, what have they not done, who they think they are, who they know they are, etc. Sometimes its unbalanced, and just strictly on academics or athletics, but the high school still tries to push the idea of being well-rounded so you are appealing to a university.

This project may create commotion but that's ok, some may feel it is stupid, and some will not believe in the areas for improvement. One thing you will not find a lot of in the next hundred pages is tons of research. Why? A study is not the final word; a favorable thesis is not always applicable to everyone. My basic philosophical thinking is, "if it works, it works." Applying educational parameters whether physical or mental means you are setting your own boundaries. For this projects purpose, I want you to expand your limits. Some sections may seem 'too broad' or 'general'; nonetheless, I want you to consider the array of ages and sports this project is pertaining to. Let's plan to keep things simple. Life is already hard enough.

However one chooses to view it, Life is a constant learning and ongoing battle. Being an athlete at any competitive level and at any age will display areas of weaknesses. Weaknesses need to be addressed to prevent injuries, mistakes, and promote improvement. In my opinion, to be a good athlete you need to balance the body, mind, and spirit for that specific individual. Each brain, heart, and body is different. To reach the highest potential for a given athlete, he or she must expand into greater areas. The mind, the body, and how the two communicate is an important topic to be discussed and an unanswered question to me. It alone sparked the creation to the first steps of this project.

Throughout my educational, athletic, and life experiences there are many people and lessons learned which have helped me. I wondered, "What have other people gone through or learned over the years, that made them stand out? What did other athletes, who achieved more or less than me, do that I did not? Who were their biggest influences? How did they think or perceive their action and/or accomplishments?" The questions never ended and that is ok. I expanded, I asked, and I searched for answers. Ironically with this journey came no answer, just a bunch of great insights and knowledge, which I felt, needed to be shared.

If you don't believe me, then I dare you to try it, because then you will believe me. It is not about proving the doubters wrong, but proving to yourself that it can be done. Nothing is impossible. Develop the mind and you can expand your capabilities, possibilities, and outcomes.

Thank you for taking the journey to become better.

Welcome to the Athlete25 Project

PART I

NUTRITIONAL

Probiotics

Not first for a specific reason, but first because you have to start somewhere. More people are starting to accept and understand the importance of gut health. Ever get athletic anxiety? What about heartburn? There is plenty of research out there linking these issues to a lack of healthy bacteria in the gut.[1] Probiotics are extremely important for the digestive and immune system. Why you ask? Both systems are directly related; it is said 70% of your immune system lies within your digestive system.[2] Your body's ability to breakdown and absorb quality nutrients is extremely important for all bodily functions.

How are you suppose to assimilate and utilize the protein shake post workout if your body is unable to fully breakdown and absorb those amino acids? How are you supposed to stay hydrated when you're

[1] Enders. *Gut: The inside Story of Our Body's Most Underrated Organ*. Print.
[2] http://www.ncbi.nlm.nih.gov/pmc/articles/PMC2515351/

chronically voiding yourself with watery waste products? How can you perform your best if your immune system is weak from fighting off all the crap you eat and your insides are "messed up?"

Just because we cannot actually see the digestive tract does not mean it is not important (Chinese medicine examines the tongue to assess this[3-4]). This may be something we all fall short on, including myself. We do not train the deeper layer muscles enough and we do not take care of our internal organs enough.

I struggled with slight tongue discoloration that hydration never seemed to fix. B- vitamins did not help, nor did other types of probiotics. It was not until my mother tried a better quality product when she informed me at how much it made a difference for her. Some things I noticed when adding a high quality probiotic to my daily routine were better rest, muscle recovery, and healthier trips to the bathroom. My tongue cleared up within about one day to a clean pink color. It gave my fiancée and I results we have

---

3 http://www.ion.ac.uk/information/onarchives/tonguediagnosis

4 http://www.shen-nong.com/eng/exam/exam_diagnostic_inspection.html

never experienced before even after trying multiple different types of products.

I would recommend something that has at least 25 billion active bacteria, preferably 50 billion daily. Since the bacteria are living, purchasing just anything off a store shelf is not always recommended. The better quality products are usually kept refrigerated. Why are they refrigerated? Probiotics are actually living organisms. Technically they are the healthy bacteria that are vital to maintaining proper health within the digestive tract.

Research reputable companies and read the actual labels in the store before you just grab anything. Considering there are trillions of bacteria in your digestive system, sticking to one product that contains a few researched strains is simply not enough. Try different products to gather an array of good bacteria in your gut overtime.

Limit Sugar and Crap food

This is almost self-explanatory; let me rephrase, this should be self-explanatory. However, it is not. Yes, I have read Carb Back Loading by DH Keifer. Yes, I understand the science behind stimulating an insulin response as an anabolic hormone for post workout purposes. Yes, I know the body needs glucose for simple cellular functions.

This is why I say; 'limit' the foods you should not be eating excessively. I am not bias to this subject because I am diabetic, because I will be the first person to tell you we need glucose in our lives and bodies. The simple fact that if you are reading this, chances are high you are an active individual who is looking for ways to improve yourself. Well start with limiting the excess of unneeded simple carbohydrates and crap food that is not actually food made of anything. Think of it this way, if it has a label on it to tell you what it is, its almost never 'food'. If you have to label a banana to know it is a banana, then we need to go back to kindergarten. Just the idea that an ingredient list has things we don't even know what it is and we must label what is in something is a little crazy. What happened to living off the land we live? We would be much healthier human beings but that's an argument for another book.

You know what is "good" to eat and you know what is "bad" to eat. Let's not be childish about this topic and create our own grey areas to get away with a box of Apple Jacks post-workout because "we are trying to shuttle nutrients into the cell." Cut back on the foods we should not be eating and eat more of the healthy stuff. Keeping the meals simple does not mean we have to eat as bland as rabbits. Steak, steamed vegetables, baked potato with a slab of butter? ALL DAY! What about two hamburgers and a box of chicken nuggets from your favorite fast food? No. Not even real meat, not even real food.

You are what you eat. You perform with the fuel you put into your body. You repair with the nutrients you feed yourself. Be smart about nutrition because it is a huge part of human life, especially in an active person who is exercising and competing at strenuous levels. You have one body to beat up and one chance to take care of it. Do not wait until you have some sort of digestive disorder or weight problem to think of changing; change now. Of course there is food that tastes better because sugar is a very addictive ingredient which is added to almost everything in some way, shape, or form.

To be a better athlete, take control of what you put into your body. Consistency will result in great long-term results. A chicken salad just on game day is as good as only practicing the morning of a competition. You can indulge once in awhile in a guilty pleasure, but use this as a reward for achieving a goal or celebrating a win. Educate yourself on "food" and start to take note what you are putting into your body.

Hydration

Good quality H2O. There is nothing better than it on earth and in our bodies. As athletes, water amount and quality is extremely important to keep our bodies moving effectively and efficiently. For proper brain signaling, muscle firing, and almost every other process in the body hydrogen or oxygen molecules are required. When you dig into the biochemistry of things and bodily processes you will see little H+ ions jumping in and out of reactions. Where do you think some of these hydrogen molecules come from? They do not just magically appear.

I am sure you have heard the term, "You are what you eat," and for this instance drinks also pass through the mouth, so they are not to be forgotten or overlooked. How much water you drink may slightly depend on the source you hear or read from. To keep things simple for the purpose of this book, just drink water. Good, clean, filtered water; not that crap from the bathroom sink. However deep you want to examine the topic, the earth is majority water, and the human body is majority water, so what do you think the majority of your diet should be? Lucky for us there is water in a lot of food sources we consume in a day. We may not see it as hydration; however, many fruits and vegetables are predominately hydrated, living foods. Isn't it interesting when a fruit starts to get old it looks "dehydrated" and shrunken. It is not because it was sitting in the kitchen for two weeks but because some of that water content has evaporated and has weakened the food structure, which now has, bruises and looks ugly. Try not to be the ugly fruit in the fruit bowl; drink your water. I can already hear a parent saying, "we need Gatorade."

Certain sport drink commercials focus on what you lose when you sweat and water simply is not enough. Without getting complicated and specifically picking out molecules in my sweat, I know the majority of the sport drink is water. Lets keep it simple and look for progress, not perfection, because too much of these sport drinks are secretly loaded with inferior sugar ingredients to make their taste appealing and the colors fun to shop with. Remember these companies are businesses trying to make money. As much money as they can create by educating the public on why to buy their product. Do not be fooled by the professionals on TV with their sponsored products because anyone around these sports on the sidelines can tell you the majority of those bottles and coolers are filled with water or highly watered-down mixtures. Believe me, I have been there; I was the guy who made the mixtures and prepared the coolers for many teams, in many different sports.

The secret is staying hydrated. When you are thirsty it is already too late. Drink plenty of fluids hours and days before. Chugging a 20oz. bottle before playing outside doesn't quite do the trick. Throw away the advertised sugar mixtures and drink the clear simple stuff. Two hydrogens and one oxygen molecule.

Sleep

Catch some Z's! Catch a lot of Z's!

Sleep cannot be emphasized enough. Good quality rest is extremely important for so many areas of life and health: hormone release, soft tissue repair, decrease stress, relaxation of the mind, etc. Most Americans do not get enough rest because life is always going, there is always something you can do or did not finish. I will give you a secret- you will not achieve the world in one day, you cannot be the best in your sport in just 24 hours. This stuff takes years. Do what you can and have to do today. Go home and sleep to prepare for the next. Being an athlete is a lifestyle, not just a daily activity. 4-6 hours is not really enough even though you can adapt to make it feel like it is enough. 6-8 hours is almost enough. 8-10 hours is an excellent range and highly recommended for those who are serious.

I can hear it now: "I can't sleep that long," or "that's 33-42% of my day," or "I have kids waking me up at

5am." Whatever the excuse is, do your best within your lifestyle to attain the most allowable rest because it is very important. Recovery of the body is in my opinion overlooked by us. We are willing to train very hard, sweat blood and tears type training; however, we are not putting efforts toward recovery in the same manner. Have to wake up at 6am? Then set an alarm at 9:30pm to remind yourself to shut down, wrap up whatever you are doing and be ready for bed at 10pm. Discipline in nutrition and training work well for many, why not use this attitude toward rest and recovery?

Think of charging your cell phone without a full charge; when you grab that phone and leave the house with 80% , this is essentially how you are starting your day on poor rest. You can make it through the majority of the day no problem, however, let that build up over the course of the week. Pay attention to how you feel, how training is going, how you recover, how much coffee do you 'need'? Now take that same concept over months, even years, and you wonder why the person who puts disciplined effort toward their rest and recovery is doing better than you?

Be smart, do what you can to enhance your outcome and performance. Take scheduled naps during the day, take a sleep supplement before bed, drink some calming tea, do light stretching before hitting the lights, focus on deep breathing to relax the mind at night, whatever you need to do. Get your rest, get a lot of it, and pay attention to how your body functions when it is fully charged.

Train hard, recover harder.

PART II

STRUCTURAL

Plane Balance

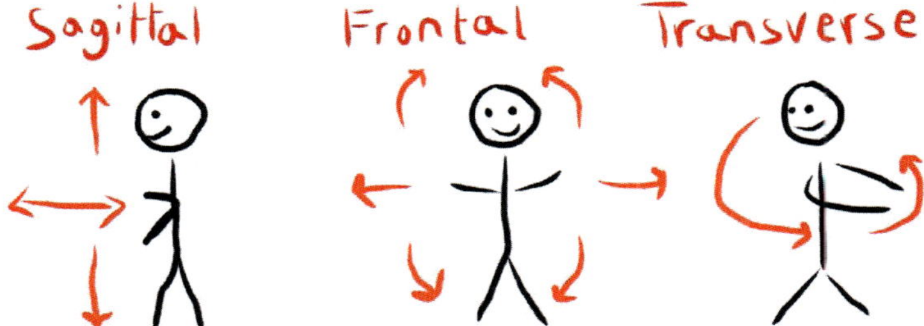

Three planes of the body made easy: left and right, front and back, top and bottom.[5]

Frontal, sagittal, and transverse planes break up the body into different regions which all require the same amount of attention. Left vs. right, front vs. back, and top vs. bottom. The body is a dynamic living piece of art. When looking at a Greek or Roman sculpture we observe curves, balance, and symmetry. It is rare to see a statue of a man with very large built

[5] http://fitforreallife.com/wp-content/uploads/2015/04/Planes-of-Motion-e1430335214471.jpg

legs and no upper body or an over-developed dominant side of strength in the creation of art. Body builders admire their hard work and ability to create balance appeasing the scrutinizing eyes of multiple judges.

When it comes to overall body motion, too much of something is never good. That goes true for a lot of things in life. Moderation is key right? Balance is ideal, but also not always very apparent until we lean too much in one direction. Too much training and not enough studying or homework and our grades suffer, too much carbs in the diet and we pack on pounds, too much work and not enough rest and the body gets tired. It is not until extreme unbalanced situations where we realize we need to work on rearranging things in our lives for improvement and by importance. The crappy part of sports is we become over-dominant in specific motions and movements toward what we do. But isn't it necessary to be great in something? To an extent, yes. Balance is key because balance is necessary.

In fact, doing the opposite of what we do too much can actually make you a lot better. Depending on who you ask or your motions of choice, eccentric control (doing the opposite motion slower) can dramatically improve the body's efficiency, strength, balance, and control. Jump a lot? Then come down and absorb the landing softer and slower. Throw 200 a pitches a day? Then have some fun and throw with the other arm for a few reps. Sprint forward everyday? Then jog backwards for a couple meters at the end of your workout.

Balance is all we need and ask for. It can save you from injuries and only help develop you as an overall well-rounded athlete. Sometimes we are so focused on our goals and working hard that we neglect to think about working smarter. Hard work pays off right? Hustle, hustle, and hustle. No one wants to see a lopsided athlete. Fencers usually have unbalanced development because of the constant stance and movement in one direction. Yes you will have a dominant side in most sports. Consider the amount of work you do for the front of your body and equal out the back of the body, the amount of upper body work and balance out with some lower body work, turning to the left too much then turn to the right some more. It is not hard and sometimes makes training fun. Pay attention to the planes of the body and motion. Please.

Posture

If you believe just because I am a chiropractor that I am bias toward this topic you are absolutely right. I have every right to be because I understand the importance of posture and why proper position is necessary for any athlete.

Look at a skeleton and you will see the body was made specifically in the shape and position it is in. Muscles are used like strong attachments to different bones with the sole purpose of moving bones creating what we view as motion. The muscles are attached in specific manners to various bones sometimes to have more than one action. In the big picture of body movement, we see one body with the capabilities of moving dynamically within its normal limits. As athletes we take this individual body and train the muscles to move in specific manners very well to become successful in our sport. We do not change the morphology of the bones and recreate how your body is put together; we simply learn a motion then develop it for strength and efficiency.

In the sport of Olympic Weightlifting positional posture is extremely important for completing the snatch or clean and jerk movements. Walking amongst the athletes you can often notice some terrible seated or standing postures of these athletes. However when they go into training or on the competition platform observe that same individual and how he/she finds an almost perfect spinal position prior to the lift and maintains this posture during the movement. Still to this day it baffles me how these athletes know what good posture is however they refuse to maintain it during normal daily activities.

The position of your body dictates your body's ability to move efficiently. A table-tennis player probably isn't really good if they are standing erect with locked knees. Each sport has its own necessary positions and posture for the athlete however when you look at the large picture of all sports, the athletic position is not very far off normal 'textbook' posture. Variations of the extremities and their angles of flexion will change the appearance of the athlete but when examining the spinal position you will view a common occurrence: good posture.

In my powerlifting days, I found a chiropractor that worked with me on restoring some of my spinal curvatures and taught me how the curves in the spine are used for force absorption. After some time of treatment and education on correcting my posture my lifts increased dramatically because I was able to produce more force and in a better, safer position. This personal learning experience forced me to assess others in different sports as I experienced this improvement first hand.

It does not matter what activity you partake in, pay attention to your position during movement. Observe your posture from the side view and front view. Breakdown images or videos to see how you move and where there may be a loss power output. The body only works as strong as its weakest link. If your head is anterior of the body the mechanics of the upper back and shoulders will be compensated somehow, somewhere. As a pitcher or overhead athlete, pay attention to the neck (cervical spine). As a soccer player or lower body dominant athlete, pay attention to the low back and pelvis position.

Sit up at the table, sit up in the chair and couch, sit up at the computer, stand tall when you walk, stand tall when you speak, stand tall and be proud of who you are. Practice good posture as much as you can so you are not staring at the floor when you get older. Practice posture when you are not involved in any

physical activity so when you are you can move and play better.

Extension

Due to awesome couches, video games, tablets, cell phones, and a little laziness, we have over-developed as a flexion dominant society. The majority of employment in this country requires you to remain seated or standing for long periods of time doing the same thing over and over again. The lack of emphasis on posture by our parents has resulted in an astounding number of people with excessive forward head carriage. Our positioning when on our phones or tablets is almost always looking down. Our positioning sitting at desk for more than a couple minutes almost always results in the chest and shoulders falling forward with the head.

The arms pull more than they press away, the legs are curled more than they are straightened, and the back is rounded more than it is erect. All these repetitive movements are happening in flexion. Flexion, in regards to the body, is closing the angle between two adjacent bones. So what can we do to help negate these issues?

Extend more and extend often. Sit up straight and stand up tall. Bring your handheld electronic devices to your face, not your face to the devices. "Text neck" is becoming an epidemic in my office with the younger generation. Parents come in with compromised flexed postures and their kids walk in behind them looking the same way. To prevent staring at the floor when you are older, start extending the spine now so it does not adapt to its overused position. Work on your extension muscles in both your lower and upper extremities. Strengthen your spinal erectors from the pelvis all the way to the neck. Referring back to the Plane Balance section, this area falls directly under that title however deserves its own emphasis.

Let's use the hip complex as an example for this idea. The strongest muscles in the lower body are your quadriceps and gluteal muscles. What motion do these muscles do? Extension of the hip and knee. What happens when you have chronically flexed hips? The opposite side becomes inhibited; simply meaning they stop working correctly. Dominant hip flexors create weak hip extensors because the extensors are unable to fire and contract correctly. Weak hip extensor muscles are a precursor to instability and low back pain. Considering the hips are believed to be the center of power generation in the body, not having the ability to extend properly and efficiently can negatively affect athletic performance.

Strong Hands, Strong Feet

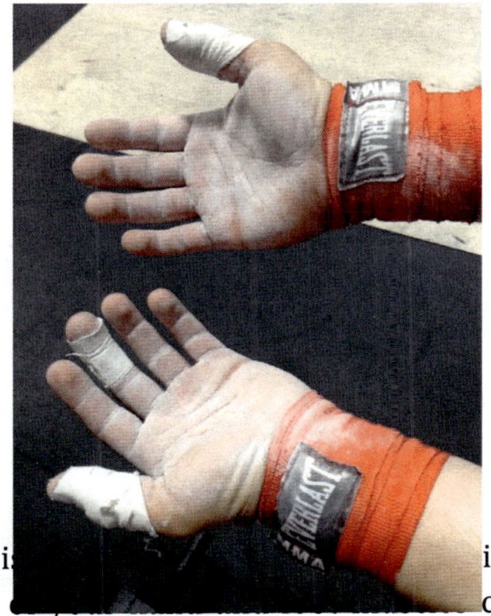

A chain i ink. Look at the size compared to your hip, leg, or back muscles. The muscles in the hand and foot are much smaller and not really as strong as the larger muscles of the body. When someone is deadlifting something heavy, without the usage of different grips or wraps, what is the first thing that gives on the person? The grip. What is more common: ankle, knee, or hip sprains? Ankle sprains. When it comes to the upper extremities, the hands are the weak link just as; the feet are to the lower extremities.

What does this mean in relation to sport? Develop your weak links to reach your full potential of your stronger links. Will the foot or hand ever be stronger than a gluteal muscle? I cannot say it is impossible, however it is not likely in the majority of athletes. One thing I have noticed through the years is every elite athlete I have met has a strong handshake. When I say strong, they do not try to squeeze the hand off purposely to demonstrate dominance over you. They simply just have a loose hand with great solid muscle development. The better the hand, the safer the wrist, the stronger the elbow, the sturdier the shoulder.

Your hand is linked with the shoulder, keep your arm straight and squeeze a fist as tight as you can while holding your shoulder with the other hand. Do you feel the contraction of the deltoid muscle? The hands developmental usage is to grab and hold onto objects to bring toward the mouth. Observe an infant; all they want to do with the hands is bring something to their mouth. Through experiences with different shapes and objects, the hand grows stronger with more dexterity. Once the hands are strong enough to grab and hold onto their bottle or toys, it is going right into their mouth. Yes, one can make the argument of teething, but why don't we stop bringing things to our mouth even after we have all our teeth, and even decades later when we lose all our teeth?

Use the same example with the discovery of feet. The child finds their foot, holds onto their foot and if possible that foot is going toward the mouth by the guidance of their hands. Once the foot grows strong enough a baby is standing while holding onto something. This helps create balance, learn proprioception, and develop single leg strength.

At some point throughout our lives we start picking shoes that look cool over shoes that function 'cool'. The shoe restricts the foot like a tight mitten on the hand does. How do you live your day with two small mittens on? The wrist and hand reduce their usage, range of motion, and will atrophy over time while taking shape to the restricted covering they are in. Why do we do this to our feet?

The feet have an extremely high amount of sensory nerves, which communicate, back to the brain. It is not surprising that people with weak feet have terrible balance and foot coordination. The feet are the basis on which we stand and ambulate. The feet are the only contact to the floor in all of land sports. Without a strong, controlled foot, the activity and motion of the person above them is not at its full potential. If feet remain grounded on an uneven surface, the knee, hip, and so on must alter their positions to accommodate for the change. If a foot is weak or unstable, what has to make up for the decrease in function? The regions above it.

Take care of your hands and take care of your feet. Work on the strength of the little muscles to assist in better moving big muscles. You are only as strong as your weakest link. [6]

[6] https://www.pinterest.com/pin/480688960198369419/

Strength and Stability Secret

The core secret is not really a secret, just an overlooked and underestimated area of the body that when worked and trained properly can have great effects on athletic performance.

The ceiling of the core is called the diaphragm muscle. This is the primary muscle in respiration as it moves up and down allowing for the lungs to fill with oxygen and expel carbon dioxide. What happens when the diaphragm muscles does not work correctly? The chest and various accessory muscles become the new "primary" muscles for this activity. Since the body is a very smart machine, the brain learns this new pattern and creates what is considered a faulty breathing pattern. The accessory muscles become very strong breathing muscles as they are now used to lift the ribs so the lungs are able to fill up. The very strong and now ignored diaphragm muscle becomes inactive, or inhibited.

Ask a few people around you to take a deep breathe and notice what moves more, the chest or the stomach? If the chest moves, they breathe incorrectly; if the stomach bulges, they breathe correctly. Are you self-conscious about your image on the beach or in a specific outfit? Do not suck your stomach in, you are only teaching yourself how to breathe wrong which becomes the start of a pattern that is not the easiest to undo. What needs to happen is neurological re-education of the diaphragm muscle, basically meaning you have to train your brain how to actively breathe again so the body can relearn the proper mechanics of inhalation and exhalation.

Google search 'diaphragm breathing' or 'incorrect breathing mechanics' and you will get hundreds of links on the how, what, and why. Fix the problem now because once you dive into learning about an inhibited diaphragm you will see issues with everything you can imagine from stress, to digestion, to headaches, to low back pain, etc.

Now onto the floor of the core, also known as the pelvic floor. This is the absolute base and foundation of the torso. The pelvic floor lies within the pelvis, which means it has a huge effect on the reproductive organs, digestion system, and pelvic alignment. Something as simple as a weak pelvic floor can alter the position of the left verse right ilium bones, which is each side of the pelvis. The change of a pelvic position can alter the length of the legs, which not only can be a cause of low back pain, but be the start to a future ankle or knee problem if left uncorrected. For more information on this aspect study the biomechanics of the lower body.

I want you to think of a room and imagine how weird life would be with a quick sand floor and/or a missing ceiling. How would you get around? How would you protect yourself from weather elements? How could one live comfortably in those conditions? Now think of your torso and imagine how anyone could be a good well-rounded athlete in any sport with a diaphragm that does not work or a very weak pelvic floor? I am not saying it is impossible because I am sure there are some professional athletes who can work on these areas, however, I am trying to make the point you will have an obvious weakness and disadvantage, which can lead to improper movements and injuries.

The core is the middle of the body; it is the important zone of force transition from lower to upper body and vise versa. Take care of your midsection on all sides, develop a stronger position in sport and protect yourself from future injuries. You cannot have a core that is "too strong" or "too stable". Find balance between strength, flexibility, and

endurance for longevity in physical activity, a healthy spine, and stable extremities.

PART III

FUNCTIONAL

Fundamentals & Perfect Practice

Fundamentals are the basic building block to all sport. By definition, according to Apple dictionary, "fundamentals are the necessary base or core, of central importance." Fundamentals in the big picture are the first skills you are taught when learning a new activity or sport. It is the way things are done and the basis off which all learning and advanced techniques are based off of.

Lets use Legos as an example[7] (because who didn't love Legos growing up)? In my basic Lego package, there was a square and rectangle Lego. Different

color Legos were included and we used them to build whatever we wanted. When you look at the finished product, you will see something made with a couple different colors throughout. The yellow, red, blue, and green legos can all be considered as a fundamental part of the outcome.

Now let's examine basketball: a new athlete learns how to dribble, pass, and shoot. Within those three areas we learn various ways to dribble, different types of passes, and special ways to shoot. As an athlete learns and develops into a player, he/she takes these fundamentals and practice to build experience and comfort with the skill. Once the fundamentals are learned the skill sets need to be practiced with a purpose. Going through the motions is not the same as trying. The amount of effort and emphasis placed on learning the right way to do things in sport is HUGE and commonly overlooked or not emphasized enough for some reason. Maybe it is our American desire of greed and fast growth? Whichever the reason, meaningful effort and perfect practice on the fundamentals in sport are necessary and should never be stopped. Professional baseball players still hit the ball off the batting tee pretty often. They learned hitting off the tee and still after some 20-30 years they still practice this activity. Elite level weightlifters can explosively get 400-500 lbs. over their head however, after 15-25 years, they still spend a significant amount of time practicing technique with just an empty bar.

Perfect practice doing the most basic movement of your sports ingrains good habits, positions, and efficiency when it comes to performance. This is one of the reasons why understanding your sport and body movement is important. Being comfortable and confident to perform specific actions is required. Repetitive actions become instinctive where it appears so easy to others that the motion appears effortless. If the swing, stroke, lift, or athletic movement looks pretty and perfect, it almost is.

Practice the basics, perfect the building blocks, and watch your athletic ability improve tremendously. The effort placed toward continuously trying to have great simple movements will transfer to complex activities. Great fundamentals can help prevent injuries and increase performance confidence. Going into a competition the athlete feels better prepared which improves their self-esteem. Keep drilling the movements. Keep practicing even when you become somebody. Have a "can't stop, won't stop" attitude toward fundamentals.

Take home message: Fun-da-mental = Mental aspects that are fun, DUH. Don't be the athlete who makes "stupid" mistakes.

Stamina/Endurance

Want to be good at your sport? Then you better start building up your endurance yesterday. Even if your activity is a short burst and then you are done, having stamina to compete is important when things go longer than expected. Better to be prepared for the unexpected.

I can vividly remember back in HS track days where my sprint coach would tell us to do longer runs or take a jog around town. After my jaw was picked up from the floor and actually realized how much this was going to suck, I began running with my team. Two miles later and after physically almost dying from exercise I realized my endurance was terrible; anything more than 200 meters was absolutely unnecessary and should be considered child abuse. I use to curse him out from across the track and hate him when I would throw up my French toast breakfast from that morning. But what happened from doing this stupid endurance running as a sprinter? Two days later at our local dual meet I ran my fastest 100-meter time and 200-meter time. How? Why? The endurance training helped my energy output, I felt stronger for longer when sprinting. The next week we did not run for any endurance and my times lowered a little bit. After that trial and learning experience I realized the importance of building stamina.

Still to this day I despise endurance or stamina work. However, I know I have to do it. Volume and repetition has me out of breathe and many times during my workouts I cannot wait to sit down and grab my sweat towel. Sometimes I even sip my water really slow with small sips just to buy time to catch my breath. But at the end of the day, these are the training sessions where you get better. You push through when you are tired, you hit new numbers and reach new levels, and you have to believe in yourself even when your mind wants to give up. You will quit before the body does. The body is stronger than you think, push your personal limit and go a little farther for a little longer. How much can you handle before you mentally quit?

Athletes with low endurance abilities are athletes who break down because of fatigue. Their technique and performance output suffers greatly, not because they are bad athletes but because they are an unconditioned athlete. Poor stamina leads to poor fundamentals and we already know how detrimental that can be to your game. Being conditioned goes a long way mentally and physically. Take endurance drills serious; add some mentally enduring sessions into your training to challenge both the mind and body for adaptation.

Stamina is just as important as, strength or power is to your sport. Maybe in a different aspect however it is still needed for improving athletic performance.

Eccentric Control

What is eccentric control? Eccentric control is basically the lowering or loading aspect of a movement. Use bench presses for example, bringing the bar down to the chest would be the eccentric movement. In baseball, the eccentric portion of a swing would be starting at your finished position and slowly winding back into your start swing position.

Why is eccentric control important? In rehabilitation, eccentric control is the best way to develop strength and retrain the soft tissues around an injured joint. Controlling the negative aspect of a movement is highly trainable and can transfer benefits into normal activity. You may sprint really fast forward but jogging backwards makes you lose balance and stability of your body with each step. Train the opposite movement and watch how you become better doing your normal activity.

An ex-professional soccer player and very successful sports chiropractor taught me how strengthening the hip extensors can greatly improve the kicking power of an athlete. This was hard to understand at first because the gluteus maximum muscle is mainly a hip extensor. However, having strong hip muscles created a very stable hip joint, which transfers to a higher force production in the swing phase. All this means is you can kick the ball much harder. The eccentric movement of bringing your leg backward into hip extension is the opposite movement of hip flexion.

Eccentric control is being able to control the opposite motion of what you do repeatedly. An Olympic weightlifter may use eccentric front squats (negatives) to control and build tension on the way down to help with catching a clean and standing up with heavy weights. The control helps activate muscles differently than they are use to which can result in better awareness of one's proprioception and the stability of their movement. Powerlifters use this technique to stress the nervous system to prepare one's mind and body for a new weight prior to attempting the lift in the future. The eccentric motion can be supported by the body better meaning you can handle more weight doing things "backwards".

Doing this type of training can also help athletes who have mobility issues by stretching the tissues in the necessary manner to train correct positioning in their technique. Consistently teaching the body the position you want it to be in while slowly entering the new range of motion prepares the joints and soft tissues for the activity.

Learn how to absorb the forces of jumping by descending slowly into a strong squat. Prevent shoulder injuries in a pitcher by starting at their complete release position and slowly returning to their start position with a light resistance band in front of them. Rehabilitate a strain of the quadriceps or patellar tendon by doing negatives with leg presses or leg extensions.

Eccentric control has been used for many years in a rehab setting but why can't we use it on the practice field by doing motions slowly backward? Lets break rules and use our brains. Refer back to the Plane Balance section for more information on keeping balance within the body. Most elite athletes will have some sort of physical adaptation to their sport that has become their 'normal'. Eccentric control will not be used in correction of these misalignments but as a stability-training tool to help the athlete's body maintain strong in all ranges and positions.

Weak? Use negatives.
Hurt? Use negatives.
Unstable? Use negatives.

Overuse injury? Use negatives.
I think we all get the point here.

Vertical Jumps

Jump high and jump often. Lets keep this simple. Explosive triple extension of the hip, knee, and ankle. Your own mass and constant gravity are the only forces against you. Your mass may vary over the years but gravity remains the same. Gravity is a controlled amount of directional force, which challenges our ability to 'beat' gravity. A vertical jump is a full body movement. It gets blood flowing, muscles firing, and the mind ready for activity. Used as a warm up drill it is great, but used as a developmental tool it is better. Excluding volleyball, basketball, or gymnastics, the majority of athletes do not jump enough. There is a lot of walking and running with quick bursts of energy and movement in between. The purpose of this entire project is to make a well-rounded athlete and improve performance.

To be better you need to do different things better and others things more. There is a reason why the NFL Combine checks on vertical leap on all its athletes. Even the 350lb linemen have to get up in the air from time to time. The ones who jump high and jump often, simply just jump better. These athletes are able to utilize their legs and kinetic energy to power through their feet and extend to impressive heights.

It is very difficult to extend into the air without fully using all of your lower extremity joints. Imagine trying to jump just using your hips and keeping your feet relaxed on the ground. Sounds ridiculous doesn't it? The quickest and easiest way to stimulate power and explosiveness is to jump. Yes, we can get technical and train plyometrics in all directions or specific to that movement, but as you read this you are probably realizing you do not jump enough and it is something you are not great at. An easy way to help yourself and your athletes is to get jumping. Reach tall and let gravity slow you down at the top. A constant full effort to always jump as hard as you can will result in sore legs and, over time, an impressive vertical. The muscular development of the lower body will set any athlete apart.

You can do jumps in your athletic footwear of choice but preferably in the most minimalist shoes possible. I like the barefoot approach or anything that allows full usage of the forefoot and toes. The body is all connected. Very tight footwear can decrease the range of motion the forefoot needs to spread, absorb forces, and function optimally.

The moral of the story is this: jump. Jump a lot. Jump with both arms stretching overhead. Some athletes jump and lead with one arm, which after many reps develops an unbalanced frame or power distribution. Personally, I cannot jump as high with my left arm leading when compared to my right arm. I have developed an imbalance and it shows in my unilateral leg strength. Ways you can improve this finding is single leg strength development and practice with jumping balanced.

Joint Effort Activities

Improve competitiveness and/or teamwork by doing things together with someone or against someone. You can only control your effort and you never really know what level someone else is working at. As an individual, a tough competitor can help raise your level of effort and energy output or you can be the catalyst to stimulate another person to work harder by trying to beat you.

In team or group efforts, training together improves communication amongst each other. As a teammate, tough challenges require working together better known as synergy. Synergy means working together for a better outcome[8]. It's a method the military uses to create trust in one another. When going into battle you know that other person has your back because of what you have been through together. Better morale with one another, better relationships, a general understanding of what

[8] According to Apple Dictionary

each of you have been through together, and knowing with the help of each other you guys/girls as one can accomplish a lot.

"There is no 'I' in team," is a popular phrase heard around the world. Push me and I will push you. A quiet, timid athlete sometimes just needs a push to get the aggressiveness out of him/her. Every athlete is different and responds to different stimuli. In a sport where focus and calmness is required, a rookie may observe one's ability to control the situation and remain focused even in high times of stress and nerves.

By visual observation alone one can become inspired or understand the level of effort required to focus and do what needs to be done. I know some of you involved in individual sports are going to say, "but I like training alone." That is fine, but do not train alone all of the time. Remember that balance thing? Every now and then push someone else to work harder or find someone who is better than you and train with him/her. In the off-season often you will find that NFL defensive backs will team up and train with better receivers from other teams to help them get better. Why? Because they have figured out if you train with others who are better than you, you can learn a lot about your opponents. Learn their tricks to the trade, motivation, effort level of training, tendencies, routines, etc.

Remember, this is a project for improvement. Do not be selfish and resort to doing everything alone and for yourself. Be open to becoming better even if it means training with the player you are trying to beat out for the starting spot. Both of you will become better in the process. The deciding factor will be who wants it more.

Penn State football players making each other better during morning workouts.[9]

[9] http://photos.pennlive.com/patriot-news/2013/02/penn_state_football_early_morn_23.html

PART IV

EDUCATIONAL

Coach

Let's start with humble; no one wants a coach who only talks about themselves and boasts and brags on where they use to be. Most coaches were previously athletes and every athlete has stories of the past. Everyone was once great and may have been better than some of their athletes. This is not the vibe you should feel or sense when taking order and direction from someone. If the coach was better than you or not, it does not matter, the coach is suppose to coach and teach an athlete about the game.

It is difficult to develop much without a coach who has walked the talk. There are plenty of gifted minds in the athletic world who were not decorated athletes, yet still great leaders with sport sense. For the purpose of this project we are trying to develop individuals for athletic improvement, not look for coaches with the best leadership ability. Having someone teach you how to squat but has not really ever squatted themselves is a red flag. Being able to squat 500lbs weighing 165lbs is not the easiest of tasks, however in the process that individual learned through experience and from other people on what to do and how. As he/she matures, they become a useful tool to others because they have done it. In my opinion, the coach who has experience is better than the coach who has knowledge. Anyone can read a book, watch a video, or take a weekend class and regurgitate it to another person. Being the guy who did it for 20 years versus the guy who read 20 books, the experience trumps the lack of activity.

An athlete must learn the sport and the best source of education is by doing. Students have teachers and athletes have coaches. A coach can be one of the most influential people in someone's life. My theory is the best coaches are the one's who can teach you about Life through a sport. In my experience the coaches who have been a big part of my athletic career were previous good athletes, educated in the activity, and connected well with who I was as a person. I was able to relate to my coaches, I was able to understand, and the simple fact of who they were had me interested to ask questions and trust what they said.

A good coach has the interest and well being of the athlete before them. They are not selfish nor search for the spotlight. A good coach stays in the background letting his/her athlete do what they were coached to do. A good coach disciplines and humbles his/her athletes to not let success or failure get to their heart and head. A good coach can adapt to situations quickly. A good coach is way more than being able to motivate or inspire another, but to educate and develop nothing into something.

Thankfully I have had the chance to meet and observe great coaches whether working as part of the medical staff or being an athlete myself. One man who I often tell others about is Cael Sanderson, arguably the best wrestler to ever walk this planet. 2004 Olympic Champion in Freestyle wrestling, 4-time NCAA National champion from Iowa State, and 159-0 undefeated collegiate record. I was a student at Penn State for his first two seasons as the head wrestling coach there and had the opportunity to be one of the student athletic trainers my senior year. Being in the wrestling room everyday with Cael and just observing what he did and how was a huge learning experience for me. I personally feel the type of coach Cael is cannot be fully described and understood on paper. When it comes to humbled and experienced, I have yet to meet or see anyone yet in my own personal life who can trump Cael Sanderson in this aspect.

I wanted to wrestle for Cael, because, well who wouldn't want to learn from one of the best, but because of who he was and how he carried himself. The way he instructed and taught his wrestlers, the way he interacted and got sweaty on the mat during practice with everyone, the way he managed himself with cameras and press everywhere looking through the windows and interrupting his practice. The way he could take other Olympic hopefuls, top Nationally-ranked wrestlers, and even another Olympic champion, to a new level. The way he was able to make men out of high school boys in a matter of a few months.

Cael started basically every practice with a quiet soft talk about sometimes things that had nothing to do with wrestling and other times just explaining his perspective on particular situations and the thought process he uses. He would remind the team of what they are doing that day, what the team could expect in the near future, and any other announcements. He would encourage the guys, give a clap or two, and in a matter of seconds everyone is off the bleachers running onto the mat to get started.

Eye contact, good handshake, and a smile was something you could expect from Cael every single day. He would take a few moments in the middle of practice to ask how I was doing and acknowledge my existence in the room full of athletically gifted beasts. Cael cares not just about his athletes but the people around him. He just has this aura that made his presence highly respected but his personality was far from that pedestal.[10]

[10] http://www.phillyphanatics.com/wp-content/uploads/2011/03/Wrestling-Cael-Sanderson2.jpg

Education and Understanding of Sport and Body

- Know what you are trying to accomplish.
- Know what you need to do.
- Know why you are doing it.
- Know how to do it.
- Know the tools you are using.
- Know the rules and boundaries.

As you have heard before, knowledge is power. Saying "I know," and showing you know are two different battles. Anyone can say anything and anyone can think they know what they are doing. As life progresses, you realize the more you learn the less you actually know. A three-time Olympian made a statement saying how he is "still trying to figure it out." After a lifelong journey in one specialty and being among the best in the world for over a decade, this athlete was still learning more about his sport than ever before. What does that tell you?

Do not ever stop learning. Learn everything you possibly can about the sport you choose to participate in. Learn everything about the tools needed to perform the sport. Become a student to your craft and analyze everything you do in respect to perfecting movement. You do not learn how to make a basket with your eyes closed, throwing the ball, and hoping it goes in. After diligent practice, feel, awareness, technique, etc. one can possibly shoot a ball with his/her eyes closed from one location just based off of knowing and controlling the variables involved with shooting.

Learn how the body moves, why the body moves, and where the body needs to be to create the movement you are trying to produce and reproduce. Understand movement in it's own form, separate from sport. Understand movement required in the sport. Use these two areas of experience to fill in your own blanks. There is rarely only one right way to do something, if you know the start and finish position there may be many ways to achieve the outcome efficiently when looking at different body morphologies and training philosophies.

Stay open and receptive to other opinions and new ideas; if you can learn one thing from someone else or another source of information then add it to your toolbox of knowledge. You do not always have to agree with others, however, being ignorant gets you nowhere but stagnant where you currently are. To grow, go in different directions to find your way. Your success and progress will not be a straight upward slope.

If you do not know, then learn. If you think you know, look deeper. Progress is a process.

Study Film

Most, if not all, team sports utilize film to study their opponents. Watch trends, formations, field/court movement, side dominance, weaknesses, play decoding, positioning, etc. This is something the smarter athletes put more focus and time in. Ask a professional football player how much time they spend evaluating and studying film. That is all you hear them speak about on interviews leading into a big game. Studying your opponent is something that is inevitable when you get into higher levels of a game.

I can remember in youth football watching film of the team we were going to play in our local Superbowl every year with the coaches. Being in $3^{rd}/4^{th}$ grade how much did I actually pay attention, read, and understand the field play of another team? Not much, but our coaches did. They would point out common findings and positions of certain players they saw over and over in different game films. This would help the coaches plan their game plan on calling formations or plays when they recognized a specific setup by the other team.

As the athletes mature and develop into the sport, this practice becomes an art. Listening to a Hall of Fame quarterback break down film and watching him explain what he is seeing and what it means is very interesting to the untrained eye/ears.

Aside from studying your opponents another aspect of studying film is watching yourself. Observing what you are doing right and wrong, why you missed a lift, why you got beat on a play, why you fell, etc. Studying yourself is one under-rated aspect of sport I feel should be utilized more. You can learn a lot about other people by studying them, someone you do not really know. However, you can learn so much more about yourself. For example, your thought process, reaction movements, instincts, imbalances, and most importantly, areas to improve.

Having a good angle on yourself can allow frame-by-frame studying of how you are using your anatomy. We can only control ourselves in movement and sport. Other people see our movement and use their own body to react. So yes, it is great to know your opponent, however, you should know yourself way better.

Like I stated before, learn everything you can about yourself and your sport. When looking at the depths and details of you and your movements there is a different motivational factor. As a health physician, I study my patient's videos to assess how and why they got injured, as well as, evaluate their progress in rehabilitation. Video tells us more than we want to know or see sometimes. The video or images are unforgiving and tell the truth behind a story. You missed the lift for a reason, you lost the race for a reason, you got caught in a reversal for a reason, check the video and learn why, then do not let it happen again. Studying yourself is an easy tool to make yourself better by being aware of the situation. As a doctor, if we know what is wrong we can fix it. As an athlete, if you know what is wrong you can fix it. Learn what you do by studying how you do it.

Change Environment to Force Progression

Becoming too comfortable in one spot will make you very vulnerable when you leave that spot. Home field advantage is good for one team when it is also a disadvantage for the other team. Why? There is comfort found in familiar places. When you go home you are comfortable, when you go to a strangers house it is unlikely, somewhat awkward, and rude for you to take off your shoes and put your feet on the table like you own it. The change in environment makes many athletes uncomfortable. This can be seen as an advantage if you train with this expectation.

Visit other fields, train with friends out of town, go to a different gym, stand in a new spot, wear many layers, alter your grip or handle, play with different speeds, you get the point. Embrace the opportunity to change the environment in which you train, embrace the idea of going somewhere new, embrace anything that challenges you.

Aside from the physical changes of elevation acclimation, before any major competitions athletes in all areas usually plan travel to arrive early with the main purpose to make comfort in a new place. They look to continue routines, energy levels, competitiveness, training schedules, rest and recovery. When it comes time for the SuperBowl or Olympics do the athletes fly in that morning or the day before? Never. A new environment affects hormones, a new diet affects digestion, a new timezone affects sleep. There is an amount of comfort needed to compete at their best.

In soccer, there are international teams that come to the US for friendly game play. In weightlifting, there are international teams that travel to another country to train for a period of time. In boxing, fighters travel to remote or secluded areas to train with minimal distractions. In football, practice fields are equipped with speakers to blast crowd noise and distractions. In all these examples there is a training adaptation that is taking place to prepare one or many for a future activity.

Not on a national team and unable to travel the world? No problem, go to your friends house, play a pickup game in a new neighborhood or park, have another player toss you a few pitches, little changes which make you uncomfortable produce a better overall you in the long run. Being in the competitive spotlight is not the easiest thing to accommodate to when it is your first time in a stressful situation or around multiple distractions. Focus is lost and new thoughts/feelings are going through the body. Add this to your training. You will thank me later.

Practice Being Uncomfortable

It is imperative you leave your comfort zone in various areas other than your environment. What do I mean by practice being "uncomfortable"? Think of it this way: improvements require change and change requires growth, whether physical or mental. To become better you have to become someone you are not today in a way you are not today.

The way I see it there are three levels of perspective, you are either getting worse, staying the same, or getting better. Getting worse is taking steps backwards, technique is worsening, and getting slower or weaker. Staying the same means nothing is changing, you are on a plateau of nothing with minimal challenges and just going through the motions to complete the task. Getting better is entering a new zone or degree. Getting better is doing something harder or more challenging. Getting better is pushing your boundaries of possible.

Getting better is not settling and accepting mediocrity. Getting better is trying to beat the you of yesterday. Getting better is simply entering the zone of being uncomfortable with the mentality of improving.

In powerlifting, the common saying on the team was, "if you are not scared, it's not heavy enough." What did this mean to us? It meant you better man up, accept the fact this is not going to feel good, and you are going to be uncomfortable. Suck it up and lift.

What can you learn from this mentality? Nothing is easy and nothing worth having is going to be easy. A personal record or new achievement is trying something you have never done before and successfully completing the task. It may mean running a little farther, faster, jumping a little higher, lifting a little more, kicking with your other leg, etc. To become who you want to be requires years of uncomfortable situations. Some shy away from challenge and do not grow or improve and others yearn for the opportunity to do something crazy. Being told something is not possible drives me to show others it is possible. What is your driving factor?

Play with the Big Boys

Being uncomfortable is not a bad thing, when you find yourself in a situation where you start to feel the anxiety of fear, breathe and focus on the task. It comes down to how bad you want it. The more you want it, the more determination, drive, and confidence will overshadow the discomfort of uncomforting. Playing with the big boys (or girls) will help this form of environment change. A higher level of competition almost always brings the best out of a player because it forces you to step it up. It's easy to dominate when you are the big fish in the pond. Put yourself in a bigger pond next time and see how you really compare to the competition.

Surrounding yourself with better, bigger, athletes is one of the quickest ways to improve your game. Do members at a sports club choose the personal trainer who looks in worse shape than they are for guidance? No, and there is a reason why they do not. You would not take advice from someone who is not in a better position than you are. So why would you surrender yourself to only practice and learn from athletes who may not be as good or experienced as you?

Jump in the deep end with the big boys. Get pushed around and don't cry about it. Get tougher and you will get better.

Adaptation

The simple evolutionary belief is adapt or die. You either get better and stronger or you do not. With challenge comes change. With struggle comes growth. An athlete must embrace the idea of growth and change. An athlete needs to understand to become better one must adapt into a better athlete. The process of adapting to training stimulus sucks, there is no way around it. There is no easy way out and there is no legal, or ethically correct way to a quick fix to make you better without putting your body and mind through scenarios where it must adapt to improve.

Adapting to a new training partner, playing surface, weather conditions, etc., are just examples of things you should not complain about and embrace. Stop the whining because you are uncomfortable and play in a different pair of shoes. Adapting to changes and getting done what you need to do is the only focus necessary. You must accept challenges in which force you to figure out a new way.

Joining a new team, playing up a level, or just playing a pickup game in a new area. Be proactive in looking for new ways to grow yourself as an athlete. Without stepping out into a new world it will be difficult to learn more about what is out there or how to handle certain situations if you own the current environment you are most comfortable with. A lack of adaptation reveals a plateau of comfort. A plateau of comfort without challenges is a great way to become and remain mediocre.

Do not let fear control your opportunity to adapt in a specific situation. Take a chance, fail, and learn. The next time a similar scenario presents itself you will be more intelligent and confident to achieve the task.

Cross Training

The idea of cross training is to address weaknesses by doing a different activity. Cross training can be seen in two perspectives: same sport or different sport. In regards to same sport cross training, use soccer as an example. The fall is outdoors on a full size field, the winter is indoors on a small field, and the spring/summer is when most tournaments occur where you may play up to five games in a 48 hour period. Each season has its different requirements upon the athlete. Outdoor play is on a larger field with longer runs and kicks. Indoor play is on a smaller field with shorter runs and kicks. Outdoor off-season play has multiple games in a shorter period of time. The issue I personally have with this approach is the activity is always soccer. Constant exposure to the same activity or stimulus, in my opinion, can accelerate the athlete's mind to become mentally drained and physically adapted.

In regards to cross training with different sports, it is normally associated as something fun to the athletes. For example, a wrestling team can play indoor soccer or dodge ball on a rest day. Athletes are generally competitive people by design so any activity they are involved in will become a game. Baseball players can have freestyle swim races on a hot summer day. This approach removes the mental stress of the game to enjoy a fun activity that actually has a positive benefit to it. A coach can use an activity, which is similar in nature; soccer and hockey, or completely different; badminton and weightlifting. The change in activity is not only interesting but also fun. It can be viewed as an "athletic field-trip", go and do something different to keep the body adaptively moving. The benefits of cross training are different usage of muscle balance, coordination, and firing patterns. The effect is physically and mentally intertwined.

It is highly recommended to let children and teens explore different sports or activities to keep their bodies developing as they mature. Taking the pigeonhole approach too soon for younger athletes increases their probability of overuse injuries in the near future.[11] Continue stressing the body with various movements and challenges to create a balanced, well-developed athlete.

All of the above subtopics are ways to progress. Progression is ultimately the goal in "getting better." According to Apple dictionary, progression is the development toward a destination or advanced state.[12]

When asked, "how can I progress?" My answer is "just keep trying."

[11] http://www.chiroeco.com/tommy-john-surgeries-overuse-injuries/76330/

[12] Apple dictionary "Progression"

PART V

MENTAL

Mental Timeouts

What is a mental timeout? Meditation, prayer, basically any moment when you disconnect from the world to search your own heart and/or mind. Mental timeouts help separate yourself from the world and everything around you for just a couple moments. Some prefer this first thing in the morning, last thing before bed, or during the day in the midst of crazy and stressful situations. Either way people know this is important for personal health reasons as well as staying focused on the goals and task at hand.

From an athletic perspective, prevent burnout for yourself by taking small periodic breaks. I am sure you have heard, "you are your own biggest enemy." It's inevitable; there will be times when you get on your own case because you did not meet the expectations you had for yourself. At that moment, take a time out. Separate yourself from the social media, from the teammates, from all distractions and embrace in a mental timeout. Encourage yourself, say positive affirmations, visualize your dream, imagine your goal, forgive yourself for the mistakes made, spend time in prayer; whatever it is you need to do, take the time to do it.

A clear focused mind is a huge positive advantage when going into training and competition. Personally, I use to take my mental breaks moments before training so when it came time for competition it was part of a habit. I was able to set the stage for the task at hand and focus all efforts in one direction. When a training session or competition did not go the way I planned, the first moment I had alone I would reflect, time out, and calm my nerves, frustration, and thoughts.

Diaphragmatic breathing is a key part of meditation. Getting fresh oxygen to the brain has this amazing effect on the nervous system. Just search the benefits of breathing and you will be surprised at how many people breathe incorrectly and how inhalation utilizing the proper musculature can dramatically change how you think and feel. Alternate nostril breathing is also another method commonly used to stimulate specific sides of the brain.

Moral of the story: schedule purposeful time outs for you in any manner that suits your needs and beliefs. Take a break from the hustle to prepare your mind, the most important part of your actions. You are what you think! "Those who think they can and can't are both right." Sharpen the most important tool in your athletic toolbox, the brain.

Remember: It's the fight **in you**, not the size **of you** that wins the fight.

Internal > External

External motivation is watching a video online, getting excited and going out to do something. Internal motivation is having a desire within to go out and get what you want. Of course there is nothing wrong with utilizing external ways to push you and give you that edge. Don't get me wrong, sometimes that comes in handy and really can make a difference in someone's day. Key word- someone's "day". In all reality, there will be days where you need to push yourself to get out of bed and do what you do not feel like doing. Not everyday will be positive vibes and extreme drive. Some days will suck.

To make a difference in someone's life the internal motivation goes a further distance. You can listen to one song or watch one video over and over and over. However, after awhile the mind will become accustomed to the stimulus and that same drive will lose its power causing the person to look for another driving force to get them going. Use caffeine for an example, one cup of coffee before a training session and you will have a good day. Repeat over a few months and one cup of coffee will not be doing much, it will now take two cups of coffee to produce similar outcomes. The body becomes accustomed to the routine, which lessens its effects.

What makes internal motivation different? Internal motivation has meaning, has power, it is the unlimited gas to the engine. Yes, a photo of a loved one is a good example of external motivation that will get you going. But the hurt and loss of a loved one is internal which drives the athlete to play their heart out. There is meaning and a purpose that is deeper than a motivating or inspiring story. When the athlete can relate on a personal level they are able to use that as fuel to the fire.

How often have you heard a story of someone who went through a very rough period in their life, which was later, used to catapult their career? We can list thousands; broken household, death of a loved one, major accident or injury, etc.

I want you to think of why you are doing what you love. What is your motivation? What gets you up at 5am even when you are tired and don't want to? What is your ultimate goal in Life and sport? Who do you want to make happy and smile by your actions? What type of example do you want to lead for others?

Spend a moment reflecting on yourself and think; are you able to get yourself going or do you need the help of someone or something else to practice? I am not saying it is impossible to utilize external aspects to help you achieve a long-term goal. However, I want to bring to light the power of self-motivation because it takes zero effort and can power the most exhausted athlete to still sprint past the finish line.

Acceptance of Failure

Losing, missing, falling short, being wrong, etc.: these are the crappy parts that come with every success story. You need to fail. You are going to fail. You will miss shots, actually you have to miss shots, and this is something that comes with honest effort. Miss to the left, miss to the right, and make the shot. If you did not fail those two times how would you know the angle, force, technique, and position to make the basket on your third try? I am sure you have heard sayings along these lines, "don't give up" and "try, try again." The key to failures is being able to learn from them. Being able to see where you went wrong, why you went wrong, and how to fix the problem to become better in the future.

Sport ignorance is missing and just trying again and again without evaluating why you are missing. There is an unexplainable natural force that uses trials and testing to teach the human species. It is almost like a cause and effect or exploratory nature of animals to try something. As an athlete, you use practice as continuous repetitions of trying. What makes the difference is the athlete who can utilize their failures and shortcomings as a positive learning experience.

Personal flashback: I have been there, I have felt the pain of losing after every effort of every day was working toward one goal. I fell short by my loss of focus, I learned lessons from my method of cutting weight, I understood more of who I was by dealing with one of the toughest athletic losses in my life. I went quiet from the world and separated myself from every family member and friend for hours after competition. I hated myself for the outcome, I felt like I let so many people down. Believe me, I have seen the dark side of a sport where I was on the brink of quitting and leaving it all behind me.

I took months off without any training, without any discussion of coming back, until my mind was clear and I was able to convince myself of not ending my competitive career in that manner. I decided to do one more competition that was going to be my last hoorah in the sport. I knew before even telling anyone or beginning to train that this was going to be my last time to leave it all on the platform. My mind was stronger and even though this would be a new challenge I was ok with my decision. I decided to no longer cut weight, move up a weight class, and go after one more state championship.

I learned how to channel my focus. I learned how to fuel my nutrition differently. I learned how to remove distractions. I learned how to use my body more efficiently. I learned how to train. I learned how to listen to my body. I learned my boundaries of when to push it and when to pull back. I learned a lot that year and I ended up with my having my best competition ever with all new personal records and another state championship title. I went out on a great note because of what I learned from my heart breaking loss the year before.

Moral of the story: Get up because you fell. Do not give up because of failure, do not throw in the towel because you are upset, and do not quit because you feel you are not good enough. Do not give up because you fall.

Learn from it.

You will be amazed at how things can turn out when you never give up on yourself. It will never be easy and no success is ever a straight path without obstacles. Keep your head up and keep trucking through, train hard and train smart. Success is a gift wrapped in failure. If you want it, you have to open it. Look to fail with the intentions to learn, because if you don't fail, that means you achieved something.

Power of the Mind

The mind is the creation and start to all action. The power of believing in yourself and knowing in your heart you can achieve something is commonly stated as step one. The idea has to start somewhere and it has to have a stable base. If you know you can make a 3-pointer, it starts with you observing the task, knowing you can do this, believing in your ability to successfully complete the shot, and then creating the action to do so. The stable base is yourself and your confidence in who you are as an athlete. Thinking negative thoughts will result in negative actions. A quote I read on social media said, "You are not who you think you are but what you think about." This resonated loud and clear with me, so I know I cannot be the only soul on planet Earth to also think this way.

Self-doubt can often lead to failure in whatever the particular area it is you doubt yourself in. Putting your mind in a state where, making or taking the shot needed is doubted, it prevents you from taking the step to act. This restricted action is a product of fear. Not only does it stem from fear; it is poison to your future. This inaction becomes a habit in decision-making. Being indecisive in everyday life is not uncommon for some people, however when viewed in an athletic standpoint, being indecisive has ruined professional careers. Athletes have lost their dream job, missed the easy shot, or gotten hurt for not taking the chances they should have for whatever reason it may be.

When you dive into the psychology of sport, the mind is a very complex aspect of competition. For the creation of this book athletes of all ages in various different sports were given a questionnaire and beyond my control, 98% of the responses mentioned something involving the mental aspect of sport. Whether it is a strength, weakness, observable trait, or important fundamental skill, everyone commented on the mental aspect of sport.

Surprisingly to me, I totally overlooked this area in preparation trying to make this awesome project when I realized I was making progress in sport more complicated than it needed to be. Each athlete is one person with his or her own mind. Their mind commands their actions. That is it! The better one can command him or herself around the playing field in the grand scheme of athletics makes them a better athlete. The level of efficiency, reaction time, and decision-making comes with experience. Consistent neural pathways, which are created, developed, practiced, and perfected.

What if we looked at the mind in the same manner? Imagination is limitless, which in theory, means the strength of your mind is far beyond imaginable. What if we created a powerful positive mind? What if we developed tremendous skill with self-motivation and self-belief? What if we practiced this mental game for days, months, and even years? What if we perfected utilizing the strength of our minds?

Be Coachable

This is an area where I struggle so I will try my best to help you. Being coachable is extremely important and for some people extremely difficult for various reasons.

I can only speak for myself on this topic. Being somewhat educated has become my biggest downfall in being coachable. Why? Because I challenge everything I hear with everything I think I know. Successful past achievements do not help, nor do a couple degrees in relatable fields. An athlete like me needs to submit to someone else who is a better "coach" and I should just stick to myself being a doctor. Trusting someone else knows better athletic technique than you in a specific field means giving them the benefit of the doubt even if you do not agree and following through with their directions. Do some athletic positions; put the body into positions not outlined in anatomy books and may at some times be seen has dangerous or unnatural? Of course! This is why all elite athletes have some sort of structural or functional dysfunction. They have adapted their bodies to their sport at the highest level. Being the analytical body movement man I am, this is hard for me to let go of and see past. However reality is, this is what makes a sport so beautiful.

Being able to hear direction, act on the direction, and consistently utilize the guidance is arguably one of the most important aspects of an athlete's growth. Being able to take constructive criticism to build you into a better person and competitor. Being able to humble yourself to the man or woman above you who taught you everything you know. Being able to alter your performance in the midst of all your focus and determination. Being attentive to someone else's attention. Being an athlete when you only need to be an athlete. Being respectful to the person or people who see more in you than you currently see in yourself.

Take home message: SHUTUP and LISTEN. Then do it.

I was fortunate to live with my coach and would often train in the garage.

Purposeful Passion

No purpose? No passion. Are you participating because you have to or because you want to? Do you practice because you are forced or because you want to get better? Let's take this even deeper, what is your purpose as an athlete? What is your passion as an athlete?

Having a purpose is the basis for action. Without reasoning as to why you are doing something there is no need for you to be wasting your time. To me passion is the fuel to the fire. When someone loses his/her passion for the game, he/she has run out of gas. He/she still has or once had a purpose, however, for some reason there is no passion and without passion, their purpose dies. Having one without the other is difficult and pretty much gets you nowhere. There are no rules as to what your purpose or passion needs to be. This is an individual decision and not even something you have to share with others if you choose not to. Unfortunately, there are some young athletes out there who are participating because someone told them to or made them do it. If no passion builds within these athlete they are the ones who will eventually leave or quit the sport.

For the purpose of this project I will be transparent and give you an insight on my personal life. Growing up I played almost every sport my township offered and truly loved participating. Met a lot of cool guys and had many coaches who taught me awesome things. Secretly I did certain things to make my father happy because he was ultimately the person who led me into the world of sports by playing and teaching me the sports he loved as I grew up. Having some athleticism I exceled in various areas and had a really good time doing so. A crossroad came where most of my friends were doing football and I was strongly involved with soccer. I would hear all these kids talk about practice and things I did not understand which made me feel left out. My dad would talk to me about football and explain the general basic ideas of the sport, which only intrigued me more.

I would put volleyball kneepads all the way up my arm and pretend there were shoulder pads. I would take any knee pads I could find and slide them up my leg to have what I thought were football thigh pads. I would proceed to throw the football in the air to myself over and over and over again while throwing my body all over the grass and dirt so my body could be dirty and my clothes or "pads" could get stains.

The next year came and I did football; I gave it a shot and had a good time. I wasn't too bad. I started as a running back and I experienced the taste of scoring a touchdown. It was a beautiful thing. But a part of me still wanted to play soccer. The following year came and I did not sign up for football again because I went back to soccer and this time I made the traveling team. I wasn't the best but I was happy. I started on the field and was pretty quick and aggressive. Later on in the traveling year I learned my father liked football more than soccer. That day I quit soccer to never return. Why? Being 10 years old, I wanted to please my dad, the man who taught me about sports.

At my last HS football game, I walked off the field on Thanksgiving Day against our rival town with the largest victory margin in the history of the matchup. I had my best day as a receiver and cried on my dad's shoulder because I knew the journey was over for me but silently him too. I participated and developed passion for a purpose that was through me but for someone else. Do I regret the switch from soccer? Not at all. Would I play football again if I could go back to the beginning? In a heartbeat. What happened? I found a purpose in making my father happy which developed a passion within to love what I was doing while I did it.

My junior year of college I was diagnosed with Type-1 Diabetes. This completely changed my life and I spent the week in the hospital planning what I was going to do when I got out. Exercise has a tremendous effect on controlling blood sugar so I created a workout and diet plan to gain all the weight I lost back. Upon exiting the hospital I had a plan and a purpose. This motivation grew into a passion, which led me to joining the powerlifting team at Penn State and then onward to Olympic Weightlifting a few years later.

My passion is motivating and inspiring others to do what they may think they cannot do. My purpose is controlling my diabetes and living a better life.

Whatever it is you do, do it with meaning, do it with purpose, do it with passion.

Believe in Yourself

Simple. If you do not believe in yourself then why should anyone else? Believe in yourself, whether it is future ability or future accomplishment. Believe in the plan and believe in the purpose. Believe in your ability to reach the goal and do what you dream to do. Believe is be-lie-eve, the lie you tell yourself before you become.

When you doubt yourself you are already guaranteeing a miss or failure. I am sure most of you have heard, "whether you think you can or can't; you're probably right." Well it is true; thinking is a process from your current mindset. If you are faced with a lift that is 105% of your one-rep max and think it is too heavy to complete, the mental aspect of fear and doubt cultivate off of each other. Before you even attempt the weight your mind has already missed the lift.

Believe in yourself before you enter an uncomfortable situation. Believe in your ability to do whatever it may be. Trust in your skill and training to have prepared you for these moments. Remove mental fear and attack the task with tenacity. If you do not try to push your limits then how will you ever know if you can do it or not. It is ok to fail, strive to fail. Remember, success is a gift wrapped in failure.

A common theme heard in various aspects of life is: commit. Commit to the lift, commit to the jump, commit to the swing, commit and believe. Believe and commit. Whichever way you want to look at it (chicken or the egg), you must believe. Committing out of hope or with a lack of effort will result in a half-ass outcome. If you want something, then believe in yourself first and foremost. No one else can do your goal or dream for you. Even when no one else believes in you, believe in yourself.

Acknowledgments

There are many individuals who have inspired, helped, donated, and aided in the process of this project:

My fiancée, Jena, chooses to put up with me on a daily basis. You let me chase my crazy dreams and hold my hand while doing so. Thank you.

My parents have always supported my journeys even if they did not see the vision I had. Thank you.

My family- Camacho's, Lopez's, Hernandez's, Eda's, Velez's, Torres's, Hall's, Weaver's, Donaldson's, Padilla's, Montalvo's. "I wish my arms were long enough to hug you all at the same time." (Lyrics from Selfish by Slum Village) Thank you.

Rob Bonora and Brandon Caroprese for keeping me realistic and grounded at times. You two have become great friends on either side of me to offer your own strengths as guidance. Always there to hear me out. Thank you.

Coach Tom Bennett is simply more than just a coach to me. Without trying you have taught me more about Life than weightlifting. Thank you.

Victoria Zurla aka "The Grammar Hammer" went through this in raw form to correct what I thought was English. Thank you.

Dr. Brett Wisniewski, Ernie Prempeh, Jay Isip, Anton Jefferson and the OLift Magazine crew, Quinn Henoch and all the Clinical Athlete providers, John Waldon at AlphaMind Vitamin Coffee, and last but not least, you.

Thank you for reading!

Made in the USA
Middletown, DE
24 June 2024

56212837R00060